The Life I've Lived

Kiltalya Washington

The Life I've Lived. Copyright 2021 by Kiltalya Washington. All rights reserved. No part of this publication may be reproduced, distributed, or transmitted in any form or by any means, including photocopying, recording, or other electronic or mechanical methods, without the prior written permission of the publisher, except in the case of brief quotations embodied in critical reviews and certain other noncommercial uses permitted by copyright law.

For permission requests, write to the publisher, addressed "Attention: Permissions Coordinator," 205 N. Michigan Avenue, Suite #810, Chicago, IL 60601. 13th & Joan books may be purchased for educational, business or sales promotional use. For information, please email the Sales Department at sales@13thandjoan.com.

Printed in the U. S. A.

First Printing, April 2021.

Library of Congress Cataloging-in-Publication Data has been applied for.

ISBN: 978-1-953156-36-5

Never Let Your Story Break You
Nor Shape You
Because After Your Wounds
Are All Patched Up,
It Will Make You A Better You

Contents

PROLOGUE 1
INTRODUCTION 5
DECEMBER 25TH, 2002 (PAST) 6
PRESENT 8
THE DAY AFTER THE ASSAULT 12
HOURS AFTER THE HOSPITAL 16
2 DAYS LATER 18
MONTHS LATER 19
A MONTH AFTER GIVING BIRTH 21
2 HOURS LATER.. 23
A WEEK AFTER MY MOM'S PASSING.............. 27
FALL SEMESTER.. 30
2 MONTHS INTO THE SEMESTER 33
SATURDAY MORNING 35
WINTER BREAK 38
LATER THAT DAY 43
DAYS LATER.. 47

SATURDAY (DATE NIGHT)	49
THE NEXT MORNING	53
4 DAYS LATER	56
LATER THAT DAY	64
EPILOGUE	69
ABOUT THE AUTHOR	73
ACKNOWLEDGEMENTS	75

Prologue

While reading this short story, you may have questions about me and my mother's non-existent relationship and you may wonder why it hurt me more than I would have expected when she passed. When I was a young girl, my mother worked a lot to give me everything she thought I needed and could possibly want, but she didn't realize that what I really needed and wanted was my mother's love and protection. I grew up feeling neglected and depressed. As a young child you are expected to feel happy with no worries in the world, but unfortunately that wasn't the case for me. I would stare into the sky and wish I was dead every night and day, I would wish child services would come pick me up and find me a new home. I always wanted a new mommy and daddy since the age of five years old. Now tell me that's not sad for a five year old to be thinking this way. Believe it or not, all this hurt and build up led me right into Evan's arms.

Evan and I met through a friend of his I was once interested in, one thing led to another and we were suddenly dating. He had just moved to the United States from Kingston, Jamaica. He had been here for a couple of months now, he was very handsome with those strong ass facial features, mid height, his skin tone kind of reminded me of butterscotch, so I knew he probably had a few girls already. In the beginning I honestly didn't care, my only intention was to be around him to get closer to his friend. The only thing I had on my mind was his friend until I figured out his type was three times my tiny size. I never planned on having sex with Evan, kissing him or anything else of that matter.

Terrible, right?

I know I know, I'm human just like everyone else. After being with Evan for two years I started to put my all into our relationship because now I love you and we're in kinda deep to be so young. We were very young but it's something about that young love that will have you thinking it will last forever. Every time he would come over to my house or I'd go to his house, there's a little gift waiting for me. He would buy me bracelets and necklaces for no reason at all. I would cherish these things and never wear them out of fear of something happening to them. At a very young age, we spent the majority of our time together. We went on dates, we would hop on the train and go picnicking in Central Park. When I was in school we talked on the phone the entire time and after school I would go see him. I was so in love with this boy nothing mattered but my relationship, I never went to family events because I wanted to be with my boyfriend. I skipped school to see him every chance I got, lied about signing up for after school programs I never attended, and whatever else I needed to do to see him. These were the good times I wished could last forever. Just when you think you know a person because of the history and years you've spent together, you find out you don't.

As time passed, we were five to six years in deep and this is where things started to become rocky. Evan wasn't the only guy that caught my eye anymore, he was slacking in our relationship and I needed special love, affection and attention to fill in the void I had inside of me from my childhood. I started to feel like Evan was cheating on me and I wasn't wrong, but I didn't have actual proof. I've had many people call me and tell me things, but there was this one particular person who was a pathological liar. I didn't know what to believe anymore or who really had my back, so I started making new friends and doing what I wanted to do for about two years. If he wasn't stunting me anymore, why not direct my attention somewhere else? I stopped caring about Evan for those two years, but then as time kept passing us by, I decided to try and take my relationship seriously again. I wanted us to work and be in love like how we were in the beginning.

Before wanting to take my relationship seriously again, you may wonder why I was so confused when Evan asked for my hand in marriage. Truth be told during the time Evan started cheating on me, I fell in love with someone I became very close with. He loved me too, but it was a type of love I've never felt before. He was older, mature, and more manly. He would pay for all my food and sneak money into my pocket every week because he knew I wouldn't take it. He even paid for nearly all my hairstyles. What girl wouldn't love to be treated like this without never having to ask for anything? My birthday came one year and he came to my job with a card and hundreds of dollars in it. He respected my relationship even though we both wanted each other very badly. He was like an angel from heaven, I guess that's why his mama named him Angel. For two years, we spent most of our free time together, we went out, I cooked and went to all his family gatherings. His family showed me the most gratitude and love in that time of my life and I loved it. They would always ask when we were getting married and having a baby. Little did they know we weren't even intimate. My body craved his body, but my mind just wasn't ready for that step. I loved the connection we had, but I also loved Evan. Angel was a man and Evan was barely a young adult and I had some choosing to do. I chose my first love because I do believe "the grass isn't always greener on the other side" and we were already so many years in and I just wanted the best love I could get because I deserved that. I chose Evan and we both got back on track with our relationship. There was a day in the beginning of our relationship, I came home from school and got a message from Evan that read:

"I know something happened to you in your life that you're not telling me and I need you to tell me when you're ready please."

I was so confused as to why he would send me that message or how he even knew that because I only smiled around him. I never really talked about what went on at home or about my personal feelings either. I never talked to anyone at all, I just bottled everything up and thought it was okay. But I wondered: Was it the silence I always gave or the way I always kept my body covered? I didn't like to be touched in any form of way, man, woman, it didn't matter. I remember saying when I was a little girl "I'll know when God sent me my future husband when someone can see all this pain through my smiles." Therefore, that's why I chose Evan over Angel, that was my sign.

Introduction

My name is Aneese Myers. My intentions in life are good. Being a good wife, good mom, and all that I can be for the people I love. Sadly, I don't see that playing out so well. You would think being in love or married is magical. I'm starting to believe that the title "Marriage" turns a couple away from each other. Is it fear? Well is it? Because I sure as hell need answers.

December 25th, 2002 (Past)

It was Christmas day and my boyfriend Evan wanted our families to spend Christmas together. I didn't understand why, but I just went along with it as I always did. The tables were set up the way you'd see a rich family dinner on television. We all sat down, had some laughs, drank some wine and ate just enough food. Finally, it was time to start exchanging gifts. Evan asked for everyone's attention as he stood in front of the room. He was smiling with joy while he thanked everyone for coming together. He then turned to me and smiled.

"Baby, I love you with every inch of my heart. I wouldn't want to live a day without you. You are the most beautiful woman I've laid eyes on, besides my mom."

"Hahahaha," everyone laughed.

I smiled while covering my face, as I watched Evan get down on one knee.

"Aneese Myers, will you do me the honor of making me the happiest man in the world by being my beautiful wife?"

I stood in shock. I thought I was dreaming. I bit my tongue to see if I'd wake up. It didn't work of course. Was I really ready to be married? I had someone else lingering around in my mind and heart, but right now that wasn't important.

"Yes, I'll marry you," I said in confusion.

That turned out to be the day I should've listened to my gut, and waited to be married. I thought I was doing the right thing because we've always talked about getting married our whole teenage years, moving in together and creating a family. That was all before we hit a bump in our relationship.

Present

"I fucking hate you asshole. I don't even know why the fuck you're still in my life."

I'm really starting to hate this man and he just cannot see how we are drifting apart. I am looking forward to leaving this relationship for my own happiness. I have to work in a few hours and with the way I'm feeling, I just want to stay in bed. Nowadays, I just go to work to get away from Evan. We can't stand each other more and more everyday that passes.

"Hello, Hello, Hey, Hey," I say to everyone as I walk into work.

I have to think about my baby each and every day because if it weren't for her, I wouldn't push myself so hard to do better. I found out I was pregnant two and a half months ago and I'm doing such a good job hiding this pregnancy. Here's a funny memory, one day he glances at me and tells me I'm starting to let myself go. Even though I live with this asshole, he still doesn't know I'm literally five months pregnant. I know it's not good to keep secrets in a relationship, especially a marriage, but I don't give a fuck. He clearly doesn't care about me, so he's not going to care for our baby either. I never want my princess to feel the way he makes me feel these days. She's already the most precious thing to me and her little kicks are what keeps me going daily. Imagine sleeping next to your husband every night and he doesn't touch you, cuddle you, or even kiss you anymore. Sad, isn't it? That's more than enough to leave or step out on your marriage, but unfortunately I'm pregnant so stepping out is not an option.

It's now eleven o'clock at night and I have class at 9:30 in the morning. The buses and trains are running at their own speed at this time and it's surely not safe for my pregnant ass to be outside this late waiting on public transportation. Three of my coworkers and I are leaving at the same time, and one of them offers to give us all a ride home. Of course I am going to be the last to get dropped off because I live all the way on the upper-east side. I don't feel comfortable giving out my address, I just want to be dropped off near my house, that way I could walk the rest of the way. As my coworker, Zayn, drops off Maria, he starts asking me too many damn questions. I feel like he's trying to distract me and throw me off track. I noticed him starting to drive on a highway that I didn't recognize, so I began to hesitate.

He pulls into this empty lot along the highway. I look out the window and look around just in case I need to run for my life.

"Where are we and why did you stop here?"

"I don't know, I just want to talk because you seem to be so stressed out lately. I just want to make sure everything is okay."

"I'm fine, I'm just tired. So if you don't mind, I'd like to get home to my bed before my husband thinks I'm out with another man."

My husband's selfish, inconsiderate ass wasn't checking on me these days, but he didn't need to know that.

I began to notice something was about to go down by the way he's staring at me. He began to compliment my skin complexion, my body, the curls in my hair and even tried to say my eyes speak to him every time we're on a shift together. I don't talk to this man if I don't have to and I definitely don't make eye contact if I don't have to. He turns and asks me why I look so fine coming to work, as he placed his hand on my knee. I ask him why he is touching me and to move his hand off of my damn leg. He reached over to try and kiss me. I slap him so hard in the face. He laughs. I'm so puzzled because I don't understand what he thinks is so funny. He quickly pushes my seat back and jumps in front of me. I try to get out of the car before he forcefully shoved my hand away from the car door. I begged him to move out of my way, so I could find my own way home, but he refused to let me out. He starts to bite on my neck and I slap him in the face every time he comes close. He gets frustrated and locks my hands up with all the force in his hands and pushes his body against mine. At this point, the only thing that is on my mind is my baby's safety. I began to cry. He foolishly asked me if I'm okay. I spit in his face as I look at him in disgrace. He forces his hands up my dress as he compliments the smoothness of my skin. I try to push him off of me, but I can see it only excites him more to see me fight. He began to rip off my panties as he unzipped his pants. I tried to push him back with all the strength in my body and all I can feel is my body shutting down. I began to cry out for him to please let me go. He tells me to just relax. I don't believe that this man is about to rape me. I even shout out that I'm pregnant. I start to beg and plead for him not to touch me.

But none of that worked, he obviously doesn't care. He continues to pull down his pants and forces himself inside of me. And that was it. The deed is done. I am no longer pure for this one man that doesn't deserve me, but nonetheless, is still my husband. I start to feel so much pain. I close my eyes and wish that, instead of reality, this is a scary nightmare that I am in. Tears fell from my eyes as I continued to ask him to get off of me. He finally removes himself from me and sits back in his seat. I am so scared and sitting in this seat crying my eyes out. I can't even scream for help, I can't say a word. I just sit here quietly while he drives me near my house afterwards. As I reach to open the door, Zayn grabs my hand and apologizes. As he's trying to explain his actions tonight, I pull my hand away from him and run out of his car and slam the door so hard, the window cracks. I run about three blocks to my house.

I am shaking so badly that I can't find my keys. Of course I came home to my husband not being there. I sit down for about five minutes in my kitchen crying. I feel so hurt, my childhood trauma is haunting me all over again and once again I'm alone. I've always felt alone and I've always been alone. Where's everyone in my time of need? It took me so many years to sleep without nightmares or worrying about someone walking behind me trying to attack me. I call my best friend Monica because she's always up and available to me no matter the time or place. She came running so quickly, it seemed like it only took her a snap of a finger to get here. She is so furious and you can hear the hurt in her voice as she calls 911. Tears start to roll down her face as if she have been assaulted tonight. If no one knows how hard it was to get where I am today, she knew. Maybe that's why it hurt her so bad to hear that this happened to me again and while pregnant. Not long after the police arrive, they take me to the police station so that I can give my statement. Then I make my way over to the hospital. My memory is starting to become blurry because I think I keep passing out from all this stress, the doctor tells me that I am not stable enough to leave. The hospital obtains two emergency contacts from Monica and they decide to call my husband to inform him that I have been assaulted. And of course he is about to find out that I am five months pregnant.

The Day After The Assault

"Baby, how are you feeling?" Evan cried out as I opened my eyes.

I knew all hell is about to break loose now that he knew I am pregnant and so far along. I glance around the room hoping to see a doctor or nurse. My main and only focus is my baby girl. I cry out for a nurse as Evan stands over me. He kisses me on my forehead, starts to run his hands through my thick curly hair and rubs my stomach while smiling.

"The baby is alright thankfully. Why didn't you call me? Who did this to you?"

I laugh, close my eyes as tears are rolling down my face, and I lay back and rub my stomach. I don't want pity from this man. I just want to go back to my life the way it was before yesterday. I honestly want Evan gone and far away from me.

"Why are you even here pretending like you care about me?" I shouted.

"I fucking love you. Are you kidding me right now? You mean the world to me and you're keeping secrets from me?" Evan shouted.

I began to cry and scream, asking Evan how could he love me. He barely looks at me anymore, as if I disgust him or something. He doesn't check on me throughout the day, he's gone all day, and he's turning into a bad compulsive liar. This is not the man I fell in love with or maybe it is and now he's finally showing me the real him. I feel so disgusted with my whole body. My mind starts to wonder and now I'm starting to feel like maybe this keeps happening to me because of something I'm doing. Is this my fault this keeps happening? Is cutting my hair all the time, wearing jeans/ sweatpants and a regular top not enough? I don't wear makeup or dress up girly daily and I keep to myself most of the time. That's no way to live your life, I should be able to show all my beautiful flaws however I want. I have beautiful medium brown skin, my eyes have this nice seductive look to them, I have very long legs and a nice body I would rather only show off at home. My blood pressure began to rise and the doctor came in and asked Evan to leave. With him gone, I could finally get some peace of mind before the detectives came back asking me a million and one questions. I roll over to go to sleep after the doctor calms me down.

It's now 3:00 a.m and all I hear is my phone vibrating repeatedly. I reach over to grab it off the table beside my bed. I had twenty five missed calls from an unknown number and ten voicemails. I put the phone to my ear to listen to the first one and all I hear is Zayn trying to apologize. Although we were leaving work, he claims to be intoxicated at the time and didn't know what he was doing. I have all the evidence I need to put this man away for a while and I plan on using it. I began to cry my eyes out and feel like calling Evan, but I quickly hit the end button. We used to be best friends, he was so over protective over me, and I missed that person. We talked about everything, we laughed and cried about everything, I'm trying to figure out what changed. What happened to us? WHAT DID I DO AGAIN?

Moments later, I receive a message from Evan.

"I know you probably hate me and I'm starting to hate me too for letting this happen to you. I am truly sorry for everything I put you through. What hurts me even more is that I know what you've been through and how it affected your life and I promised to never hurt you. I failed you and allowed someone to feel like my wife doesn't have security at home. I'm sorry you felt like you had to hide a pregnancy from me. I couldn't wait for us to have a baby, but not this way. This was supposed to be something special for us, not just for you. I'm supposed to be at every appointment, talking to my baby girl before work and after. You deserve flowers, foot rubs, massages and much more. I'm sorry I've been missing out on everything I'm supposed to be a part of. I'm sorry I'm never home anymore, I ignored you and took you for granted. I swear you are the best thing that ever happened to me. You were always the only one I could count on and you were the one that held me down when I had nothing and was going through my surgeries. I remember a few years back I thought you were going to get tired of me and leave me, but for some reason you stayed with me all this time. I'm beyond grateful. I love you with all my heart and promise to be the best husband and father from this day on. I hope you can forgive me even though you don't owe it to me, but it would be a blessing."

I began to cry because it was all too late. All this pain and confusion has got me and my baby tired as hell. What am I supposed to do? How am I supposed to feel?

He didn't protect me and he wasn't there for me. Instead he was avoiding me and never came home. Damn man, how the fuck do you let this happen to your *wife*? I am not your girlfriend, we didn't just meet, I am your WIFE. We were best friends, I've never done no disloyal shit to you, so why do me like this?

I close my eyes and wait and wait for time to move faster. I want to be out of the hospital right now.

Hours later the doctor informs me that my husband is there to take me home. I asked her if I could go home alone. She said if I wasn't in danger, I would have to go home with him.

Just when I thought life was going to get much better, this shit happened to me. I am willing to give up my vows and leave the man I loved dearly. Now, he doesn't even want me to pee in private. I wonder why men wait until bad things happen to be who they first were once again. My mama always used to say, "You better fix it before God fixes it."

I never listened or paid any mind to that statement. But now, with all the fighting and arguing Evan and I have been doing, I'm guessing this is how God plans to fix us. And I won't even bother to question God.

Hours After The Hospital

KNOCK, KNOCK, KNOCK

"Who the hell is knocking on my door so early in the morning like this?"

Oh no, this asshole called my mama. I was so happy to see her, but also so furious. She rushes through the door as I open it, hugging me like it would be our last time seeing each other.

"What'd they do to my baby?" she cried. "And what's this about you being pregnant and keeping it a secret?"

Last time I checked I am grown and paying my own bills, but maybe I'm bugged out.

"Sometimes it's not good to speak on your blessings, mama."

She looks at me like she wants to slap me and hug me at the same time. This is a conversation I just wasn't ready for. I didn't tell her about it because our relationship isn't that great either. It took me many, many years just to build a relationship with her for reasons she doesn't even know. My mom was diagnosed with cancer when I was in high school, it made me want to be closer to her regardless of what I felt towards her.

"We just got home from the hospital, she probably needs to rest right now mama."

I look at Evan and roll my eyes. I just want to slap his yellow face blue.

"Ask Evan where he was while I was getting fucking raped," I mumbled under my breath as I walk back to my bed.

My mother looks at me in confusion. She doesn't know half of what we'd been going through in this house. For all she knows we're this happy loving "Husband" and "Wife". But it doesn't matter, because as long as my baby is fine, I'm fine. At least that's what I keep telling myself.

2 Days Later

"Hey, hey, hey, where are you going?" Evan shouted as I tried to walk out the door.

"I have a sonogram appointment my dear, now move please."

"You don't think that's something I would want to be a part of?"

I looked at him and rolled my eyes. He quickly threw on some clothes and we headed out. As we're sitting in the car, I see tears running down his face and he turns his face towards the window. I start feeling bad because now I'm starting to feel like I'm being really hard on him. I know he's not processing what happened to me clearly. Especially knowing I'm pregnant with our baby girl. I know that had to fuck his mind up bad. He couldn't help me. He wasn't there to protect me. I lean over and kiss his cheek and tell him I love him.

He holds my hand from the time we step out of the car to the time the doctor calls my name. Luckily my baby was big enough for the doctor to see her through my belly. I wouldn't let them do a vaginal sonogram under any circumstances right now. Evan has the chance to listen to the baby's heartbeat, and he gets to see her moving around. With all this mess going on, she was smiling a lot today. I was really surprised, but it makes me feel really good. There's no more secrets to hide now. I feel really relieved. After leaving the doctor's office, we walk to a cafe up the block for some lunch. There are things we still need to talk about.

Months Later

"I'm off to work now sweetheart," Evan calls out as he kisses me on my cheek with his soft lips. I smile and watch him walk out the door. When he promised to be a better husband he must have meant it because he's giving me everything I've always deserved. He wakes me up out of my sleep with kisses, I'll wake up to him staring in my face smiling or doing something that'll make me smile. He even comes straight home from work and we go for long walks. For so long we've fallen off and real bad, but now I finally have my sweet husband back. This lets me know that people can really change, I just wish it didn't have to take a bad situation for change. It's time to prep dinner before I get back in bed. As I walk to the refrigerator I start to feel water leaking down my leg and suddenly a pain strikes me badly from my back to my stomach. Today must be the day my little princess is ready to come out. I slowly drop to the floor and began screaming and yelling out Evan's name, hoping that he would hear me. I sat and cried, trying to stay as calm as I could. I know many females' water can break and they still are in labor for over 24 hours, but I've been a little too active throughout this entire pregnancy.

I'm happy to hear keys wobbling in the door. But instead of Evan, it's my mama once again. Within the past couple weeks she's been here for me more than she ever has in my whole life. I'm grateful that Evan snuck and gave her a copy of all the house keys. This is a perfect time for her to pop up without calling. She see me sitting on the floor, wondering what's going on.

"Why are you just standing there looking like you don't see what's going on? CALL THE AMBULANCE!"

She runs to the phone and dial 911. Moments later she comes running towards me with cool towels for my face.

"Just breathe Aneese, it's going to be alright. They're coming soon, just sit tight baby."

We'll have to call Evan on the way to the hospital because he's long gone. I'm in so much pain, but all I could think about right now is Evan and I being parents. I knew I would make an amazing mother, but I have my doubts about Evan being a great father. Will he be a great dad to our baby girl? Will he protect her, make her smile and feel loved? Will he make promises to her that he knows he couldn't keep? I don't know, but I do know it's time to practice my breathing for the last time.

Evan shows up just in time because it's time to push little baby Trinity out. One moment I feel like I'm going to die pushing this little girl out and the next moment when her head finally pops out I was okay. I was lucky to have my mom and my husband next to me throughout the process. This baby is the biggest blessing of our lives and she's what's going to bring us all closer together. Given the circumstances, we deserve her regardless of anything.

And there she is, Trinity Harmony Bailey. Born August 26, 2010, 6:52 p.m, 7 pounds and 10 ounces. She's so beautiful, with a beautiful caramel skin tone, and curly lengthy hair. This is really our little innocent child and I love every inch of her. My world suddenly starts to feel whole again, and I start to feel happiness in my heart. I have my big butterscotch and my mini butterscotch.

Giving birth to Trinity brought back the light I'd been missing for so many years. It was time to make better decisions for the future of our child, but right now I'm going to enjoy being a mom for the next few months.

A Month After Giving Birth

I get a message at 11pm at night about none other than...my husband. We'd been doing so good lately, spending more time together, and starting to love each other more. As I see these messages coming through on my phone, I feel like my heart dropped down in my stomach.

"WHAT THE FUCK IS GOING ON NOW?" I cry out.

Honestly, I feel like I'm about to go crazy right now. Some bitch is texting me telling me that she's pregnant by my husband. How he told her before that we were getting a divorce, but he disappeared over a month ago and now she's looking for him. I have been living in positivity for a little while. I've been happy, smiling, and not fake smiling either, I gave this man a beautiful daughter and I've been a great wife from the start. I guess nothing is ever enough. I'm going to sit in this living room and wait and wait for Evan to get in this house. I need answers and I need them FAST!

A few hours pass by and I finally hear keys wobbling in the door.

"Aneese, I'm home my snuckums."

"How was my two favorite girls' day?"

I give him the side eye with a full blown attitude.

"What the fuck I do to you now?" Evan yells in confusion.

I throw my phone at him for him to look at the messages.

"So I'm guessing this is where you were in all of my time of need. This is why you couldn't even tell I was pregnant or even unhappy with you, HUH?".

I'm so livid just looking at his fucking face. All I feel is rage, and a tad bit violent.

"I can explain, just give me a chance to speak."

Just when I thought life was getting better, it came crashing down all over again. This pain cuts deeper than being raped. I assumed something like this was going on, but having actual proof is even worse than assumptions. I feel disgusted and betrayed. I can never in this lifetime trust him ever again. There's no way I can forgive him for this. There's just no possible way.

"You're mad at me without knowing if this bitch is lying or not, but how do I know if you actually got raped and didn't just lie for attention or something, HUH?"

I look at Evan in disbelief with tears in my eyes. I couldn't understand how he could say something so hurtful like that to his own wife to cover up his cheating? What's next, Trinity is my rapist's baby?

"You didn't notice I was pregnant, five months pregnant at that, but you knew someone else you were giving all my love to, was pregnant. You were there for her, you went to the first few appointments, and was taking pictures with her and her baby bump. You're going to sit here and think I'm going to lie about being raped like this is some sort of joking matter to cover up your shit. And I sure as hell didn't call you when I got raped because you are worthless trash, the hospital did. Is the hospital in on this lie too?"

I walk to Trinity's room to sleep in the nursing chair next to her crib with the door locked. At that point I don't know how much more I can take. I've been hurting my entire life, and at this point and age, I did not deserve any more pain. I know now, in my heart, that it's time for a divorce. There's no coming back from this situation. I don't need to hurt, I don't need to cry, I don't need dark circles around eyes, and I sure as hell don't need him. He needs me, let's not get that twisted.

2 Hours Later

I get a call from my aunt saying I need to hurry to the hospital. Something happened to my mom. My world is now completely crashing down on me after it was all coming together so beautifully. I began to pray on my way to the hospital that everything is okay with my mom. When I finally arrived, I could see all the sad faces and tears in everyone's eyes. As I walked closer to my family I began to cry because the energy in the room told me all I needed to know. My mom is dying before my eyes and she had the audacity not to tell everyone. Maybe she thought she was Jesus and can just heal on her own. But this is not the time to be upset. I have to tell my mama how sorry I am for missing out on all those years for what I didn't tell her. How could she have protected me when she couldn't find out what was going on with me? She always told me a mother knows, but how could she have known and done nothing? I guess that's where a lot of my anger came from. She would always think she knew what was going on in that house, what was going on with me or even in my head. My mom is being taken from me and Trinity too soon. My heart is beyond broken and right now I can't bear this pain I'm feeling. I took a moment to breathe and go talk to my mother's almost cold body. I hummed her a lullaby as I ran my fingers through her scalp. She wasn't always the best mother, but she was my mom. There's so many things we didn't get a chance to do. God blessed me with a beautiful angel to do what? Take away my mother.

Now that mama is gone, my body, mind and soul is numb every day that I wake up. I know I have to stay strong for Trinity, so I decide to pick up a pin and piece of paper to write a letter to my mom. I'll leave it at her plot at the graveyard on the day of the ceremony.

"DEAR MOM,

I know you're in a better place, but I miss you a lot. We never got the chance to talk and discuss the conflicts of my life. We never talked about how you let that man get away with what he did to me. It changed my life in ways you'll never understand. I never understood why it happened to me. Why did it happen to me? Why does it happen to others? Why does rape exist? Every man that hurts little kids deserves to die. I always wished bad things upon you. NOW LOOK! YOU'RE GONE. I cry day and night while yelling, "Come back." But I know there's no coming back. I truly wish RIP meant Return In Peace. I wish we could've settled this situation. It's hard to forgive and even harder to forget. How can I forget if every time my husband touches me I get jumpy or scared? How do I explain this to him? I didn't know how he'd take it. I don't know how daddy hurt his little girl and allowed others to join in. It hurt so badly.

He had to plan to harm me that whole day. He bathed me, took me to my room, didn't even have enough sense to dress me, but told me to go to sleep. I laid down wishing you were home, but you weren't there to hold me, dress me or even tuck me in. I got up and put on my night dress, then went back to my bed to go to sleep. I thought I was having a bad dream when I felt a sharp pain in me as I was laying still in my bed. I kept hearing noises and I realized I was crying. Someone was hurting me, very badly and I was scared. Suddenly, I opened my eyes to see the man who's supposed to be my protector, hurting me. My room was very dark and cold. All

I could hear was my bed creaking and me crying. Calling for my mommy, but you weren't there the night I needed you the most. He had his friends over and they were not much help either. I was alone, I was confused and scared. The only question I had for that night was, WHY ME? What did I do? He took something precious from me. Something that belonged to my husband. I can't even begin to understand how someone can do something like that to their own child. And would even go so far as to let their friends join in. They all took turns and wouldn't stop. He must've cleaned me up really well and threw away all the evidence so you wouldn't find anything just in case I told. He never told me not to say anything. Did he think I was too weak to say anything? I needed you so badly and you just weren't there. It's not your fault though. I still loved you and will always love you. Everything happens for a reason, I guess. I miss you a lot and wish you were here. I just wrote this letter to free my soul. I love you always.

Love your daughter,

ANEESE"

It's not easy getting over the death of your mother, especially when the relationship was rocky all your life. Writing this letter to my mom makes me feel better in a way that will no longer cause my body to break down. I still have to deal with my husband having another possible child on the way. Have I not been hurt enough this year God? Have I not? Going through tough storms like this makes me wonder what could he possibly have planned for me and this life I'm living.

I've been raped for the second time in my life, I just lost my mom, and my husband was apparently out making a new family before he left his own. What am I being punished for? I'm a loving, decent person, even after all the trauma I went through as a little girl. Why do I have to be an adult and keep going through this bad stuff? What did I do, God? What is it? Or what is it I'm not doing? At this point in life I feel like God has some explaining to do because this is crazy.

I am beyond broken at this point. I don't know where to turn or what to do anymore. I don't know who to trust, who else to love, or what to do with myself anymore. What I do know is that I have to move out of this house. Sometimes strong people get tired of being strong. I know I'm ready for someone else to be strong for me, but how I look at the world is that it's a bad place and so are the people in it. Time to get up and call my girl Monica over so we can go apartment hunting while this idiot is at work.

Today is the day I think I found the perfect place for Trinity and I. It's affordable and just perfect for the next few years. I put down four months rent and the security deposit once I find out that I've been approved for the apartment. I hurry home to start lightly packing some bags and hiding them in the back of Trinity's closet.

A Week After My Mom's Passing

A week has passed and I finally have the keys to my new place. For the past three days I've been sneaking out loads of clothes every time Evan leaves for work and on the third day, I sit on the bed and write him a letter letting him know that I'm leaving him, I want a divorce and I'm pretty much done with our marriage. I change my number, so that he won't be able to contact me. As the days pass by, I notice a missed call from three days ago. I listen to the voicemail and it's a man saying he was my mother's lawyer. I quickly call the number back to see if he has some important information I should have known about my mom. He said that my mom had left something for me when the cancer started getting worse. I rush my ass over to his office the next day with a racing heart.

Hm, Hm, Hm, Oooooooou child, the news I received today from that man is breathtaking. Where the hell did my mother get a hundred grand from? I am beyond shocked that my mother left me a hundred thousand dollars, but wait there's a note attached to this money.

> "I knew, I knew and I'm sorry I didn't take legal action. He was drunk one night and I walked in on him talking to himself about that night. I handled it. I'm so sorry I wasn't there for you like I

should've been, but no mother would think her child's father could ever want to look at his own child in such a sick way. You were supposed to be his princess, someone he loved and protected, not hurt. This was totally my fault though, I've always known something was totally off with that man. My plans were never to create a family with him, when you're young and being dumb you make bad decisons that lead you to make bad choices. I should've come to you and handled this instead of letting you be so angry with me for all these years. I hope you can finally open your heart to forgive me. I know I don't deserve that, but please forgive me for your own sake. You are an amazing young woman and you deserve nothing but happiness and great wealth. You can not be happy and extremely angry at the same time, you'll take so many years off your life baby girl. What I'm about to say to you next I hope it helps ease your pain a lot more. I'm the reason why your father is dead. That night he was talking to himself about what he had done to you, he only had a few more hours to breathe. I'm truly sorry I didn't tell you sooner, but I just couldn't risk it at that moment. I love you with every inch of my heart.

Your Mama"

This hurts me to the core. Now I know why she allowed me to be upset all these years without pushing a mother-daughter relationship on me. She allowed me to come to her on my own timing. All these years I have been so upset with my mother and didn't get enough time to enjoy her while she was alive. Today's a new day and I'm an amazing person.

I'm pretty much settled in my new home, I feel good and I'm a lot more at peace. I don't have any man stressing me, I don't have to answer to anyone and I get to enjoy my beautiful princess.

As Trinity took her afternoon nap, I began to think deeply into starting a blog. I feel like I can help others try to heal. I was brutally raped as a child and as an adult. I didn't use either situation as an excuse to act up throughout my teenage years or my adult years. I don't smoke, I only drink little sips of wine occasionally or a little rum here or there and I'm very well educated. One more semester and I'll have my PhD in psychology. I'm proud of who I am today. I can proudly say that aside from the men who've raped me, I've only been with my husband sexually. My trauma only made me want to grow up and be great. I've been angry for so far too many years. Now I deserve to be nothing but to be happy. I don't go to therapy twice a week to still be miserable.

Fall Semester

I found the most pure hearted person I've ever met to help watch over my baby girl while I got back on track in school for the last semester. I came back to school with every intention of starting a #MeToo club. Sometimes it only takes one person to speak up for hundreds or thousands of other rape victims to be brave enough to open up too. I will be accomplishing everything I worked so hard for while helping other people like me heal from their hurt and anger and most importantly, being the best mom I can be. By the time my daughter gets to the age where she has a better understanding of many things, I want her to look at me as a great role model. I want her to be proud to call me her mother because I'm so amazing in her eyes and the impact I'm making in the world is awesome.

Monday morning, I go visit my counselor to pitch my idea for this new club and get some feedback on the steps I should take. She's thrilled with my idea and tells me she's here to help me with the process. I quickly pull out a pen and a piece of paper and make a list of ideas.

MY IDEAS FOR THE CLUB

1. Open circle warm up
2. 15 minute Free write/ draw
3. 10 minute meditation

4. Fundraisers for a group trip once a month
5. Bake sales
6. Building sisterhood
7. Create a free space for all genders
8. Make sure everyone leaves in a better space they came in

I have so many great ideas to get the club started. After my last class I ran to the computer lab to work on flyers. I'm super excited to be doing this. Finally taking a stand and sharing my story I thought I'd take to the grave. While I thought about my idea, something told me to download Instagram on my phone even though I don't know anything about Instagram. I want to make a #Metoo page for the school as well. Why not go all the way with this?

All the sexual assault pages I came across didn't have many followers or traffic, but I won't let that discourage me at all. My #Metoo page may just turn out as something huge. I'm not really looking for a crazy amount of followers, I'm looking for silent, scared victims of all ages and genders who need someone to talk to and a listening ear. I want people to know that someone understands their pain, their confusion, and will listen and support them one hundred percent. Especially young people.

A few weeks into my #Metoo movement, I already have ten people attending the club and 35 followers on Instagram. I try to be very active on this page and I have everyone in the club follow the page as well. I've noticed many girls under the age of 16 reaching out to me. Some stories are more heartbreaking than the others and the way I break down and cry my eyes out. I don't know these girls from a hole in the wall, but I understand that pain and it's not something you can sleep off or forget about. Hopefully throughout the semester or at the end, some people may be comfortable with sharing their story with the world. If not that's fine too, no pressure.

As I'm up past midnight typing up this essay, I hear a notification ring on my phone. YAY, an Instagram message.

"Hi, I just wanted to say thank you for creating this page. I am 14 years old and have been molested once at 12 years old by an 18 year old boy and another time for about 7 months straight by a close friend because he would never listen to the word no. I never thought I could tell anyone or get through the shame I felt until I came across this account. Because of this page I stood up for myself and made the assaults stop by relying on someone else to help me that had been through the same thing. Sexual assault is a real problem everywhere. Thank you so much for putting awareness out there for victims."

My heart was so warm by this message, my spirit felt so good. A few weeks of posting sexual assault awareness and a few videos has helped someone overcome their fear of silence. This is just the beginning and I'm ready for what's to come.

I've been so happy for the past month that I forgot all about my meeting with this divorce lawyer. Hell, I forgot I was still married. Life has been so great for me and Trinity. I haven't spoken or seen Evan since I left that house. Do you know how free I feel? I feel like a bar of Irish spring soap right now.

Today is the day I get l to sign these divorce papers. Honey, all I know is this man better sign these papers and go about his business like he was doing throughout our marriage. I wish this could be my very last time seeing this man's face, but unfortunately we have a child together. I am so glad I'm getting this divorce because I can feel success coming my way soon and I don't need anyone trying to take pieces of what I work so hard for.

I am officially a free woman and I don't think I'll be dating any time soon. I am now in a relationship with my #MeToo movement. The commitments I've been giving to this club and the Instagram page is wonderful. It's been life changing for me in many ways. I'm used to being behind the scenes and staying silent. When you keep your faith, even through the bad times, watch how good your life shifts. I promise you the devil thought he had me, but I can assure you I got away.

2 Months Into The Semester

We're halfway through the semester and I'm ready to have our first bake sale on campus to raise money for #MeToo's first trip. I'm thinking we can go ice skating as a team bonding experience. We'll have lots of fun, some of us may fall on our asses a few times, but we'll keep getting back up as life teaches us to do. First, we need to focus on these exams coming up. Study and ace every single one of them, that way, this trip can be an end-of-half-the-semester celebration. The aim is to build trust among each other. Even when I leave and graduate, I will forever and always be there for each and every one who needs me. I've spent my entire life being antisocial, but this feeling of being social is amazing.

Every other day messages were coming in heavy on the Instagram page from young girls. These stories I'm reading and listening to made me so sad, the more I read the more I cry. It makes you wonder why are we not watching our girls the way we're supposed to? How come all these children are going through this kind of abuse? Are their mommies working to give them everything like mine was? I would never really know, but I'm here to pick up the pieces I didn't throw down. I'm just happy to be their listening ear. I even share my own stories, how it affected me in life, and share every obstacle I've had to face to get to where I am today. Let me tell you, it's not that easy to process this type of trauma. Not everyone heals from it or even talks about it, they'd rather take it to their grave and die in misery.

I still have many other things to deal with in my life. I have a child with someone who has rights to her as well. I've kept her away from him for months before the divorce. Life really sucks when you're in a situation like this. It was supposed to be "Mommy, Daddy, and Me" not "Mommy, Eric, Daddy, Shay, and Me". I've always dreamt of having a solid family, but then again those were just dreams and only dreams. Right? I did everything right and with time, it all turned wrong. It happens to the best of us.

Saturday Morning

Today's Evan's day with Trinity. Boy oh boy, Lord knows I do not like seeing this man's face. I can't take the look of regret and sadness he puts on whenever I see him now. I don't even speak to him unless I'm reminding him of something pertaining to the baby. I get in my car and drive off. I don't want to hear the bullshit, I don't want to argue, and I just don't think it's time to have one of those conversations I feel like he wants to have. Keep your sorry baby, I'm sure this whole world is just as sorry as it looks. This is my time to run and do some errands while Trinity is with her dad. Next stop, the grocery store.

As I walk into the grocery store with my shopping cart, someone rudely bumps into me. Look here, I've been feeling good all day, I don't need anyone trying to mess that up.

"Watch where the hell you're going idiot."

"I'm so sorry, I was about to lie and say it was an accident but it wasn't."

"So, your plan was to come to the grocery store and get beat the fuck up today?"

"Hahaha, you got jokes I see. No, but I saw you get out of your car and I was amazed."

Oh hell no, I say in my head with laughter.

"Can I get your name? Can I be your friend, not your man, but your friend?"

My name is Aneese, I have a newborn, recently divorced with so many other things going on in my life, you still want to be my friend?"

"I asked to be your friend, not your husband. It seems to me you can use some positivity in your life and I have a lot of that. By the way, I'm Alex."

We both laughed and he followed me around the entire store while I shopped. I haven't had male contact like this in a very long time. I've only known you for what, an hour, and I'm totally down to being your friend. There's no harm in friendship. We exchange numbers and go our separate ways. I go do the laundry, put away the clothes, and freshen up because it's been a long day. I sat down with my phone to see what's going on in the world and noticed Alex sent me a text twice already. I don't want whatever this is, getting out of hand or to be taken out of context, so I wait about six hours before replying, that way it's nearly bedtime. It's 10:30 p.m and my phone rings as I get out the shower and look, it was Alex calling. I smile while answering the phone. Why am I smiling so damn hard right now, I have no clue. We talk all night long, by the time I look at the clock it's 2:00 a.m. Enough is enough now, I have to go pick up Trinity in about another 8 hours, so I wish Alex a good night even though it's morning already.

Things with Alex are too amazing, it scares me and we're not even in a relationship. He asks how my day is and wants to know how I'm feeling everyday, all day. It's a good feeling to have someone care about how I feel for once, but I can't get too distracted. I have a human to tell all my secrets and feelings to and he either understands or try his best to understand.

I finish up with all my classes today and I have a little free time before it's time to go home to my baby. As I walk out of the school building I see Alex standing out front. I laugh and ask what he was doing here. He wants to take me to get some lunch. I guess that was his excuse to see my face again even though we talk over the phone and FaceTime nearly everyday, but that's not really the same. Other than Monica, I've never had a friend like this, shit Monica and I don't even talk this much. I need this in my life right now, my mother's passing still feels like it was yesterday every now and then, and I'm divorced with a child.

    He's always helping me study after school for these finals. We go to cafés, diners and even the library because it's less of a distraction. I'm starting to ask myself what's the catch with this dude. You're handsome, very intelligent, such a positive person, and the list goes on and on. Why the hell is this man single and secretly chasing after me? Who sent you sir?

Winter break

*L*ord knows I couldn't wait for this break to come. I finally agreed to going to this cabin with Evan so he can spend more time with Trinity, but under my supervision. As long as he stays out of my way and my business I'm fine with this. The entire drive to this cabin I decided to sit back and admire everything from out the window. It's so beautiful up here and the snow makes it look even better. This only proves the world is a beautiful place, it's the people in it that makes it ugly. We enter the cabin and take a tour around the place. First thing I check for is how many rooms were in the place. I will not be sleeping on a damn couch or in the same bed as my "ex husband". And I say ex husband with emphasis because I'm petty like that when it comes to him. We take off our coats and I get Trinity all comfy and fed. She basically slept the entire ride up here so I know she was hungry and needs changing. It's time to sit down and catch my breath. I picked up my phone to let Alex know I made it here safely before he starts texting down my phone. This is kinda like family week so I'll talk to him when I get back home.

    I turn on the television for some baby entertainment for my princess, Evan's over by the fireplace trying to burn some firewood for a fire, and it's time to get some food cooking. We stopped by a grocery store on the way up to buy a week's worth of food for the week. I could go for some damn tacos with a lot of sour cream, but my tongue kinda wants some oxtails. Hmmmmm, how about I make them both or have ground beef and oxtail tacos. It sounds weird, but why not have fun with your food and keep trying new things out. Who knows, this might one day make me millions of dollars. I cut up peppers after putting the oxtails on the stove, turn my music on medium and sing along to it. As I'm singing and moving my hips along to the music, Evan comes trying to sneak up behind me. We haven't even been here for 24 hours and you're already trying to be too friendly with me. No, no, no sir I don't know who raised you into thinking you can do whatever you want and that's the way it's going to be, but do not touch me.

"Please don't mess up my mood, stay your distance please. Give me twelve feet at all times like we're in a pandemic."

"Why do you have to be like this to me. I know things ended sorta rocky, but it didn't end that bad for you to be treating me like I'm nonexistent."

"Right now you are and right now that's how it's going to stay. I don't need you or nobody else trying to break down my spirit ever again. It feels good to go to sleep and wake up happy every single day. Do you know how good that feels? I'm sure you do though, you were waking up happy everyday in our last days together while I was waking up sad, hurt, depressed and pregnant. So happy that you couldn't even see that I was pregnant, now that's the hilarious part right there."

"Wow so this is what you're going to hold over my head for the rest of our breathing lives? I made a mistake, I disrespected our marriage, I'll admit that but it's never going to change the fact that I'll always love you and my daughter so much."

"You don't see me cooking? Go entertain Trinity, isn't that why we're here. Not to be some big ass happy family again."

This is not one of those times where you think shit can go back to normal because that's what you want, I don't think so my brother.

I thought I would be cool with coming here, but now I'm starting to feel like I'm going to regret all of this. This is too much and I'm not really ready for the family trips and hanging around each other, like shit is all cool between us. The Bible tells us to forgive and forget, there's no one in this world who can forgive and forget. I don't care what anybody says. It's either or to be honest. A few hours pass and the food is finally ready. Just smelling the food is making me even more hungry than I already am. I take out two plates so that I can share the food out for me and Evan to eat. I unpack all the strawberry and banana food for Trinity so I can feed her a little something before I begin to eat. As I'm sitting here feeding Trinity, all I could think about are my petty ways. I just want to enjoy this week and get back home to my personal space. I walk back to the kitchen to reheat my food, I suddenly remember I bought four cans of frozen piña colada's mix for this trip. I had an entire bottle of rum packed in my suitcase before I even packed my panties. I go pour a half bag of ice into the blender, I look over and just that fast see Trinity trying to fight her sleep. I take her out of the chair, give her a quick bath, and rub her little body down with some baby oil. She was out in no time, I gave her a few goodnight kisses on the cheek and made my way back downstairs. I walk back to the kitchen to finish making my piña coladas and trust and believe I packed my fancy glasses for this trip. As I'm reheating my food, I walk over to Evan to offer him the drink in my hand, he smiles at me and takes it. It is definitely movie time, I ask Evan to find a movie for us to watch as I walk back to the kitchen for my food and drink. I come back to the living room area to see he chose a scary movie to watch, he knows I don't get scared watching horror films. I sit down and place my food and drink on the coffee table in front of me until I'm comfy enough to dig in. I sip my drink three times before biting into my food, I think I might've poured too much rum in this drink. Oh well, I'm still going to drink it and maybe go for a second glass. This is my time, Trinity is asleep for the night and if she wakes up, that'll be Evan's problem. While we're here I will not be getting up out of my sleep if she wakes up crying.

We're sitting on the couch for nearly forty five minutes in silence watching this movie and I caught Evan staring at me several times. I look over at him and say,

"If you have something to get off your chest, this is your chance to do so now, while I'm intoxicated and willing to listen."

"I'm just grateful you agreed to come up here with me and allow me to spend better time with our daughter."

I look at him and smile.

"I'm over being hurt, upset, and holding on to bullshit that can either break out my beautiful milk chocolate skin or that'll make my beautiful thick hair fall out. Stress and depression kills my brother."

"But still, I never meant to ever hurt you, I never wanted our first child together to be conceived like this either, I pictured everything differently and the turnout was very bad."

"Things happen even when we don't know the reason for them, but what will never sit right with me, are the things you said after I thought things started getting better."

He moves closer to me, grabs my hands, stares into my eyes, and apologizes with so much sadness in his face.

"I forgave you already, that's why we're here, now move so we can finish watching this corny movie."

The movie is over and somehow we both fall asleep on the couch together. The last thing I remember is me telling him to move after talking and him moving over, but I wake up in his lap. I quickly get up to go check on Trinity and she's still sleeping. I wonder what kind of night she had that she's still sleeping. I use this time wisely to go freshen up before my luck runs out. As I'm in the shower I'm beginning to reminisce back on the conversation Evan and I had last night. I'm trying to think of everything I wanted to say to him after I left the apartment we once shared, so that I can get it all out now and stop being such an asshole to him. We have a daughter together and are going to have to co-parent forever. I would like to be more friendly in the process. I grab my phone so I can multitask, shower and make my list for tonight.

After getting dressed, I go downstairs and warm up the breast milk I've frozen for this trip, then I go wake up Trinity because I don't want to mess up her sleeping schedule I have put together. I feed her, then sit her in her chair and start breakfast. Evan finally wakes up and goes freshening up before acknowledging either one of us. He then comes walking in the kitchen, kisses Trinity on the cheek and makes her laugh by playing with her a little. I'm finishing up the eggs, he comes behind me and whispers good morning in my ear. I laugh so hard because why are you whispering in my ear like there's a house full of people here and we have to sneak and talk? During breakfast we discuss our activity plans for today, it's very cold out and we have an infant so we have to plan wisely.

Later That Day

Today was such a great day for all of us, it kinda feels like we're a family again, but I'm not giving that too much thought right now. I haven't really checked my phone since I got here. I go get my phone, I want to see what I'm missing out on in the social world. Of course I knew I would have a message from Alex.

"Hey hun, I miss you already and hope you're having fun, but not too much fun lol."

"Good morning beautiful lady, I know you're having family time, but I'm just checking in on you."

Immediately I start smiling really hard because it's just something about this dude that makes me blush like a teenager. I can see Evan watching me from the corner of my eyes, that made me laugh even more.

"Is there a reason why you are staring in my face sir?"

"Is there a reason why you are smiling so damn hard?"

"Yeah I got some messages from a friend that made me smile even though it's definitely none of your business."

"A friend? What friend? Monica?"

"Um no, his name is Alex, we met the same day your visits with Trinity started and have been friends ever since. He's really nice, surprises me after school and helps me study."

"Wow so basically yall date? Is he around my daughter when y'all linking up?"

"I knew that was coming, no he's never been around her, and we're not a thing either."

I'm trying to figure out why he's questioning me so much, yes we had a little conversation, but that doesn't give him no reason to try to be all in my business.

"Don't you not have another baby on the way or something? All in my Kool-Aid like you don't have your own jar to be in."

"Whatever man, you don't know what you're talking about."

I take out some meat for dinner and go sit on the couch so I can play with my daughter and tire her out. I love looking at this little girl, I still can't believe I carried a baby and gave birth to a beautiful, healthy baby girl. I'm really a mom, I get to dress you up, take care of you and take you all over the world with me. The greatest thing I got out of me and Evan's entire relationship. I'll forever be grateful for the seed he planted inside of me.

I sang Trinity a lullaby until her eyes closed, then put her upstairs to bed. I have to get some things off my chest, I grab my book to do some writing. I walk into the next room with my drink and my book and start writing down all my feelings. I'm writing down everything I need to say to Evan and I'm going to have a few drinks so that everything can come out straight. No holding back nothing. This drink is getting to me a little and making me think about Alex a little. I run downstairs so that I can at least start the stew chicken and leave it on low while I take a relaxing bubble bath in this beautiful bathtub. While running my bath, I sit in the bathroom debating if I should call Alex. Instead I text him so I won't look thirsty.

"Pssssssssssssssssssst."

"Lol, you okay?"

"Yes, I'm starting to miss you now!"

"Wow, you must be on something that's not your usual glass of wine because you never tell me you miss me."

He FaceTimes me and I answer with the biggest grin on my face. He could obviously see I was tipsy. We're talking, talking and I feel like he's starting to notice I want him, want him now. I wish I was home right now so I could be next to him. We have been on the phone nearly 45 minutes before I start hearing noises outside the bathroom door. I know Evan's standing by the door listening, I said Goodnight to Alex while calling him baby. I rinse my body off and make my way into the bedroom and who do I see sitting on the bed?

"I thought he wasn't your man, liar."

"You sound hurt for not minding your business. Funny thing is I would understand if we were still married, but we're not. What do you want from me, you want me to be all dried up and single for the rest of my life while you're out here humping on A-Z?"

"I want for you to give me a second chance. We can start fresh and I can show you how sorry I am instead of repeating myself. And why do you think I'm this dirty ass guy that sleeps with all these women? I made one mistake."

I began to laugh so hard that tears started coming out of my eyes. This was the funniest joke I heard in a while and I hear jokes almost everyday.

"Second chance? Did you take a sip of my drink or drink the rum straight from the bottle? I won't give you a second chance if Trinity could open her mouth right now and ask me to. You're nasty and you disgust me."

"Why not though? Look at our history and how long we have been together. Please stop calling me nasty, you're going off assumptions and not facts."

"I looked at our history before I decided to actually leave you. I don't want your other pending bundle of joy at my house under no circumstances. I don't want that chick coming around with no bullshit or laughing at me. No sah, No way, sorry."

"Aneese, that baby has been born for a month now, I wasn't at the birth, but I did go to the hospital to take a DNA test. Before we came up here I got back the results."

"Okay and…….. this has nothing to do with me."

"I'm not that baby's father, Aneese damn. Can you stop please for once in your life? She lied and somehow contacted you to get under your skin, so that you would leave me and with the thought that she could have me."

"She could've had you, I don't care. This doesn't make me feel no better. You cheated on me with a hoe and now you think telling me you're not the dad is going to make me take you back. Hell no, I'm happy with where I am with Alex. And maybe when I get back home, I'll let him come spend the night to finally make me feel good. If that was your baby you would not be in my face trying to get your family back right now."

"Wow I really can't believe you just said that to me. If you're trying to hurt me more, you've accomplished that when you left our apartment months ago and when you signed them papers."

I get up to go put on some clothes because I'm tired of this conversation now. I made up my mind about what I want when I get back home and it sure as hell wasn't Evan this time. I've learned from my mistake the first time I chose him over someone else I wanted so badly. As I walk towards the dresser for my clothes, he grabs my arm and pulls me back on the bed. This time it wasnt to talk. He lays me down, starts kissing all over my body, he kisses my lips so softly, looks me in my eyes and keeps apologizing. Look, I'm drunk enough to give in to whatever is about to go down right now. It's been so long since I've had sexual contact, shit I think the last time was when Trinity was conceived over a year ago. All this talking I did with myself and look at what's happening right now, I'm here making sweet love with my ex husband all night long. Don't judge me, it's been a very long time for me, so why not? It's just a little harmless sex, right? I know when I wake up in the morning I'm going to seriously regret this, but for right now I'm going to enjoy every bit of this moment. He always knew exactly what to do with my body so it's worth the slip up.

Days Later..

For the remaining days in that cabin, I slept in the room with Trinity trying to avoid Evan as much as possible. I cooked and wrapped his food up, I stopped offering him drinks and I had Trinity eighty percent of the time so I wouldn't have to make too much eye contact with him. When I woke up in his arms that next day, I was so confused about life all over again. He held me like he used to hold me when we were first in love, my heart was warm, and I kind of felt completely whole again. I was grateful when he kept his distance from me after that night because I needed it. I don't want one night to affect my future again. For some reason I'm starting to have thoughts about putting my family back together, but I need more time to think about that. One day at a time. I still have a few weeks left before I go back to school. I'll continue to drop Trinity off to Evan on Saturdays like before this cabin trip happened. I have a dinner date this Saturday coming up and even though Alex already likes me for all that he has seen already, I still want to make a great impression. I feel like this will be the start of something new and good for me.

These next couple of days I'm going to spend my time focusing on the girls and planning our first activity together for next week. I create a group chat for group trip ideas and since it's just females in our circle currently, we'll plan girl trips together. What I've learned in these past few months is, being social is so heartwarming for someone who has been antisocial all her life and feeling like I never needed anyone. I love having friends, I love being understood, and most of all hanging out with such amazing people. I've always felt misunderstood, and instead of people trying to understand me and figure things out, they'll rather talk about me. I had to train myself to never care what the next person said about me or I'd be a depressed person. If someone has nothing nice to say about me, it'll never phase me, but I bet my reaction will bother them.

Saturday (Date Night)

Today's finally Saturday and I'm super excited. My eyes open up around 9 a.m this morning, the perfect time to get up and pack up Trinity's things for the weekend with her dad. I go pin curl my hair up before pumping extra milk because you can never over pack for an infant. Time to wake Trinity up, bath her, feed her and get her out to her out the door. I go slip into some leggings, a lazy day sweater, and my comfy boots.

As I'm parking my car to pass Trinity over to Evan, I see him staring all in my face once again. If I had a dollar for everytime he gave me this look I swear I'd be rich by now. My guess is the pin curls gave it away that I was going somewhere. I got out of the car and started laughing at him.

"What the hell are you looking at?"

"Obviously you, but what's the occasion because that's the only time you wear your hair all silky and curly."

"What's with all these questions every single time you see my face? You are wondering what Aneese is doing and what she's up to 24/7 now, damn. If you had this energy a year ago, we would still be married and together. But If you must know I'm going out on a date tonight with Alex, time to get back out there since I've been kinda single since before our divorce."

"Wow, I give you space and you took it to go out with another dude? Then you say this with so much pride, you think it's cute to try to hurt my feelings every time you see my face?"

"I didn't need to take your space sweetheart, what happened in the cabin was a mistake and I had a weak moment. It was just sex and that's all it's gonna ever be. And don't get me started on hurting feelings because I'd miss my date talking about this subject."

"Wow Aneese, have a nice weekend and please remember what you just said to me."

I walk back to my car laughing my ass off because why not? I just sit here for a complete minute before driving off. Damn, why must I always be like this to this man? I can't help but to not laugh at his pain after all he's put me through. I find this behavior towards him very amusing, but then I start feeling bad for him. Yes we all make mistakes, but I feel like he knew better and more than anyone. We talked about everything, we've done everything together, if he felt like he wanted to step out on me, then come to me and talk and let's figure things out. He didn't have the respect to do that, so now he's going to have to deal with how I treat him until further notice. Today's the day I noticed that no matter how many times I tell myself I forgive Evan and I'm over all that's happened between us, I'm really not. Even if he tells me why and explains what led him to do what he did, I would still be upset and won't accept his apology until I'm truly happy and moved on with someone else. I don't know why I'm dealing with this situation this way, but I'm trying to stop. This is what you call toxic behavior and honestly I don't need no more of that in my life ever again. As a person who's trying to heal from whatever trauma and issues I'm dealing with, toxic behavior is definitely not going to help me heal from anything. I know better, so I should do better.

I rush back home, so I can start going through my closet about a million and one times. I feel like I want to wear a mid-length dress but can't decide which one. Do I want to wear something sexy with heels or do I want to wear something decent with boots? I get to my closet and pull out a nice pair of jeggings jeans instead of a dress. I can definitely put something fabulous together while throwing on a pair of booties with a thick heel, do my makeup, and make sure my curls drop perfectly by the time we arrive at the restaurant.

My doorbell rings seven o'clock sharp, I ran to the door to let Alex inside, put on my coat and we were out the door. First thing he did was compliment my whole appearance, as if he didn't believe it was me. I love to keep it simple on a regular day, I'll wear my hair in a high messy bun, but most of the time I throw on one of my caps, I wear jeans or sweats, sweaters, and sneakers. I don't care too much for nails and makeup either unless the occasion is special, three days later I'm biting them off, but I do love my regular little manicures and pedicures.

While at dinner, we talk, laugh a little bit, and stare into each other's eyes all night. And at the end of it all, Alex snatches the check and would not take no for an answer. His reaction over the bill made me smile. I'm so used to paying for my own food and being super independent that this feels good. After dinner we take a little walk before getting back into the car. We talk some more and laugh for about twenty minutes. He turns and looks at me and asks me how full I am, I look him in the eyes and tell him we're not going for any more food. We walk back to the car and he drives to this ice cream place I wasn't familiar with. Lord knows I'm trying to get my body back snatched before next summer and he's trying to fatten me all up by spoiling me with so much food and dessert. We're having such a great time, so I'll let it slide for tonight.

We get back to my house and I invite Alex inside for one of my amazing drinks. It won't be wine and they won't be as strong as the ones I made at the cabin either. Let's just say we won't be blaming anything on the alcohol tomorrow. I think I learned my lesson for sure two weeks ago. We walk into the house, I take Alex's coat and hang it up as I point to the living room area for him to make himself at home. I run to my room, kick off my shoes, and slip into something a little more comfy. I don't know how this night is going to end, so I go wash off my makeup and brush my hair up into a pretty curly ponytail. Can someone please tell me why I'm staring in this mirror smiling like I just hit the lotto?

For once in a very long time, I'm starting to feel appreciated and I love this feeling. I put on my favorite house slippers and ran to the kitchen to start these drinks. Look at him just sitting over there trying to find something for us to watch without me asking him. Evan always asked me if I wanted to watch a movie with him, he never just turned a movie on and said, "Babe come on let's watch a movie." That asshole. I take some popcorn out the cabinet to pop for the movie. And just in case these drinks somehow are too strong, the salt on the popcorn will balance the alcohol out. I walk over to the couch with the drinks in my hand and the popcorn bowl in my mouth. I'm not moving from this spot until it's time to go to bed, so hopefully I got everything we need right here. Alex sees me trying to place the drinks down without spilling the popcorn, he takes the drinks from my hands and sits down right next to me. Thirty minutes into the movie I lay my head on his shoulder and pretty much cuddle up next to him. I love the way he smells, even with being out all day he still smells like he just got out the shower. He grabs my hands, kisses me on my forehead, and puts both arms around me. I look up at him and ask him to kiss me on the lips this time. He laughs and gives me a little tap kiss. Do I really want this? I'm not sure, but we're about to see. I get off the couch, sit on his lap and start kissing him some more. He didn't stop me, instead he kisses me back and rubs his hands up and down my back. He then pulls my ponytail for my head to jook back and starts kissing on my neck. Kisses turned into little bites. Oh my god, this shit feels so good. I can tell this is going to be a magical night that I will not regret. I spent my entire life doing what I thought was right and that led me to getting cheated on, assaulted, and divorced before thirty. And don't forget the part where I have a child and have to co-parent with someone I can't stand to look at anymore. I deserve every second of happiness this man is giving to me right now in my life.

The Next Morning

As I open my eyes. I see an arm around me and feel a body pressed up against mine. Last night definitely was not a dream. I quietly slip out of bed and make my way to the kitchen so I can get some breakfast cooking. Twenty minutes later I go wake Alex up for breakfast. You can tell I enjoyed my entire day and night last night and felt very thankful when I opened my eyes this morning. I'm all about presentation when it comes to my cooking and pretty much everything else, the way I set the table up with all this food will make Alex look at me in amaze. I made bacon, sausages, turkey bacon, scrambled eggs with cheese, grits, biscuits, cinnamon rolls, and waffles. I wasn't sure what he wanted and how he would wake up feeling about breakfast. I put on a pot of coffee, take out orange juice and apple juice and sit it on the table. You can never go wrong with a little bit of fruit either. I notice how wide Alex's eyes open as he enters the kitchen and looks over at the table. I laugh so hard and believe me it wasn't that funny, but I didn't expect his eyes to open up that wide.

"Are we having guests for breakfast or something?"

"No, we're having breakfast for two."

"Do you see how much food you made for two people?"

"Look, I didn't know what you wanted, so I made a little bit of everything. Be grateful, sit down, shut up, and eat what you can before you ruin breakfast for me."

"I'm more than grateful, I'm actually amazed right now because it doesn't get anymore better than you. I apologize if I made you feel unappreciated."

I smile and sit down at the table so I can eat something while the food is still warm. I'm starving and food doesn't stay hot forever, especially breakfast. We eat breakfast in silence and afterwards I head to the bathroom to shower. Alex comes in after me kissing on my back. I tell him that's enough kissing for one occasion and I'm not trying to get my hair wet right now. It's a process to dry thick natural hair and nobody has time for that right now when my hair is all silky and nice. After getting dressed, we kiss each other and part ways in our cars. I miss my little angel and I know she misses her mama too.

I knock on Evan's door this time, instead of waiting in my car. It's not too cold out, but I want to be a little bit nosey and see what he's done with the place since I left. He comes to the door with a "What are you doing here?" look. His face expressions are always hilarious. I push my way through the door and walk inside to see everything just the way I left it. I'm guessing that's why trinity doesn't give him too many problems, her room is exactly how I left it. She must feel at home when she's here.

"The way you looked at me when you saw it was me knocking on the door is hilarious. Like you had someone up in here and got scared."

"It's literally too early for you and your shit for real. I look at you with all these face expressions because I never know what Aneese I'm going to get today. Is she going to be nice or is she going to be an asshole?"

"You made me be an asshole to you, so whatever dude."

"Okay and I've apologized a million and one times, but that means nothing to you. Enough is enough, we're not children, I'm not kissing your ass anymore nor will I keep apologizing. We're not statues, we are humans, we live, we learn, and make mistakes. Not once did you allow me to make up for mines, so why keep trying if I'm not going to ever get anywhere?"

"You must've forgotten when I forgave you before Trinity was born and not long after having her, you allowed someone to disturb the peace. Then wanna come tell me you don't know how she got my number, she got it from your fucking phone. Only God knows how many other people you've been sleeping with all this time."

"If you would have truly forgiven me, you wouldn't have walked out on me like that. Not today Aneese, we all have problems and deal with them how we are fit at the moment without thinking of the consequences. Look at what you're doing, sleeping with this friend of yours because you think you have it all figured out."

Even though me and Alex finally did sleep together last night, I wasn't going to tell Evan that. I walk to Trinity's room to get her ready to go home. Next week will be the old routine, come outside, get Trinity and I'm driving off without a word. He's obviously getting too comfortable again.

4 Days Later

For the past few days, I spent my time planning a skating trip for the girls and I. What better way to work on team bonding and trust than to go skating together and break up into groups while trying our best not to fall. I'm very excited for this day because I finally get to be social and positive at the same time for once. Not long after the babysitter arrives I get a call from Evan. This is not a good time for him to be calling while I'm in such a positive mood. Trinity is not supposed to see him for another two days, so why is he calling me? I answer my phone and ask him why he is calling me if it's not his day with the baby. He asks me if we could all go out to dinner tomorrow night and tells me I could pick the place and time. I agreed to dinner and told him I have to go right now before he starts another conversation. Tonight is my night with the girls and I want to give them my undivided attention all night. I kiss my baby on the forehead and rush out the door like time is running out. I love to be early and on time, on time, so that just in case someone arrives before the given time, they wouldn't be standing outside alone waiting for the rest of us.

As soon everyone arrives, we all head inside, get our skates, and break up into groups of two. I explain the rules of the game I made up and assure the girls it was okay if we fall down, as long as we get back up laughing. The laughter would be great anyways. We break up into groups and start skating around. Eventually I turn my head to see how everyone is doing in their groups and all I see is smiles. Some are having conversations and laughing. My heart starts to feel warm again, this is a great experience for all of us. Throughout the small sessions we had before the break, some of the girls were still shy and didn't talk too much, but now look at everyone. People on the outside can look at us and think we're just a huge group of friends skating, when some of the girls are just getting to know each other for the first time. Once everyone is done skating, we all huddle up and decide on what food we all want to eat. I've been eating so many crazy foods, I'm going to get a fruit smoothie. I tell the girls we have about twenty minutes to meet back at the skating rink. It's still early and many of the girls may not want to go back home just yet. Luckily for us, the skating rink has an arcade on the other side. I walk towards the shop across the street for my smoothie and notice one of the girls running behind me. Her name is Rachel, she is one of the sweetest people I've ever met. I slow down and let her catch up to me. We walk and talk because I notice the look on her face isn't the same look she had while skating in her group. I have an eye for when someone has something to say but don't really know how to say it. I ask her what's going on. She explains to me that she doesn't want this night to end. I look at her and smile.

"We're not ending the night just yet. After we eat we'll go to the arcade and play the games for as long as you girls want. Here's our chance to act as childish as we want."

"That sounds really fun, but why have all this fun and go home to chaos afterwards? Seems like a waste of happiness to me."

From the things she's told us in the group sessions, I start to feel kind of bad for her, so I suggested we all go back to my house and have a sleepover. I will set up the living room with blankets and pillows and we could watch a movie or find something else to do. There's light flashing in her eyes and it's incredibly bright. Letting the girls sleep over at my house is better than letting them roam the streets trying to avoid their houses. We walk back to the skating rink and I gather everyone together and ask everyone how they would feel if we all went back to my place and had a sleepover. All I hear is a lot of loud yeses, that was enough for me. I promised we would go to the arcade. I tell them to go play for thirty minutes while I make a call. I call Alex and tell him I need help with a few things.

"Today was me and the girls' first outing together and some of them knew the day was coming to an end and the faces I saw I couldn't resist."

"What do you need me to do?"

"If you're not busy can you run and pick up about ten night dresses for me and I'll pay you back when you get to the house."

"I don't need your money, do you see what you're doing for these girls? You're a student as well and you're acting as if you're their counselor or something. This is really amazing and I support it. I'll be there in thirty minutes tops."

"Thank you so much and please don't buy anything pricey, it's for one night, I know how you are."

"Whatever Aneese, just text me the sizes and I'll see you soon."

I love this man, he's always there when I need him and when I don't need him. I gather the girls up and we make our way over to my place. By the time we get there, Alex is already in front of the door waiting with bags. I give him a kiss and open the door. I direct the girls to the living room, show them the bathroom for changing and anything else, and release the babysitter. Alex offers to stay and help with Trinity just in case she tries to wake up at any time. I am not about to turn down this offer.

I go freshen up and get into something a little more comfortable. I do have two bathrooms, which is now beneficial to have. The girls fresh up one by one some two by two and I start making little snacks. Look at Alex over there picking out a movie for us and nobody asks him to. I don't think he'll ever stop amazing me. I lay out snacks, juice and water for all of us. I turn to Alex to kiss him goodnight and he whispers in my ear telling me he'll be waiting for me. I laugh and walk towards the girls. We all cuddle up together under our blankets and get comfortable. Not long after the movie starts, I start seeing some of the girls falling asleep one by one. I've never had sleepovers and so many females in my house all at once, this right here made me feel great. Every time I see someone's eyes close,

I would smile until the last person's eyes were shut. Rachel is the last to fall asleep, five minutes before falling asleep, she turns to me and whispers "thank you". I quietly get up to make sure everyone has a blanket over them, I go check on my baby, and walk to my bed. Alex is laid up with my favorite pillow and he knows that's my favorite pillow to fall asleep with, but he also knew I wouldn't just snatch it from under him. That's how I know he purposely laid down with the pillow. I pull the blanket back and lay down under it. Not even a minute after laying down, he turns around laughing behind me.

"Did you notice I took the pillow?"

"You know I did Mr. Funny guy."

He put his arm around me and started kissing all over my back. I'm tired, but he came running when I called. I turn around and start kissing him. He turns me around the opposite way and whispers,

"You have a sleeping baby in the other room and a living room full of guests, don't make too much noise."

I try so hard not to laugh, but I couldn't hold it in. He's making love to me like Evan used to. As time is passing by and we're still going at it, all I could see was Evan's face and suddenly it was over. We both fall asleep shortly after sex. Hours later, I get up to pump milk, make a bottle, and check to see if Trinity needs changing. It took me by surprise when I saw her eyes open, but she's laying there very quiet and just staring at the ceiling. I pick her up, change her, and feed her while walking her around the house. I have a house full of guests this morning, so that means I can cook breakfast the same way I cooked breakfast last week for Alex without him asking if we have guests coming because they're already here. I reach for the tablet in the dresser, sit Trinity down in her feeding chair, and start breakfast. I'm someone who likes to make breakfast first then wake everyone up to it.

The food's done and four girls had already woken up in the middle of me cooking. Time to wake up the rest of the girls, so we can all eat and get ready to start our day. Here comes Alex walking in the kitchen smiling at me while greeting everyone around the table. After eating breakfast, some of the girls leave in pairs to go home and Evan offers to drive the rest of the girls home. I go look for my phone because I forgot to charge it last night. Evan texted me this morning and tried to call me. Damn, I almost forgot we have plans later. I sent him a quick message letting him know we'll be ready at seven o' clock sharp tonight. I clear off the table, wash the dishes, and sit down on the couch for a little while. I turned off the baby's tablet and began playing with her. Even though I'm still kind of tired, I don't want her to rely on technology growing up so it's my job to physically entertain her. I gently rock her back and forth like she's a little delicate airplane, I tickle her with two fingers and she laughs her little self to sleep. I lay her down in the bassinet I keep in the living room and rush to the bathroom. I have about an hour or so to take a shower, brush my teeth, brush my hair in a nice bun, and pick out an outfit for us both.

After my shower, I brush my hair for five minutes straight trying to figure out why the hell Evan kept popping up in my head last night. I grab my tooth to brush my teeth and hear someone knocking at my door. I rush to the door as fast as I could because my baby is sleeping in the living room and I need her to get her full nap today while I get us ready for tonight. I look through the peephole and who do I see again? Alex.

"You're back?"

"Yeah, not happy to see me? Damn, was the sex bad last night?"

"No babe, I'm just tired."

"Well, lay back down and I'll take you guys to lunch a little later. How does that sound?"

"Great, but I can't today, I'm sorry. We have plans tonight with my daughter's father."

"Oh, well that's great, you guys are getting along better."

"Um sure, if that's what you think. I just cursed him out a few days ago."

"You have to stop arguing with that man, you guys have to co-parent in peace and positivity for your daughter. Please try to stop being so negative towards him. Now come give me a kiss, so I can go home and think about you all night."

He grabs me close and kisses me a few times and heads home. I go back to the bathroom to tie up my hair and finish brushing my teeth. I walk to my closet and pick out a pair of jeans and a nice dressy shirt with a blazer. I walked over to my jewelry box and took out a necklace that Evan bought me about six years ago. Lets see if he remembers he bought this for me. After laying our clothes on the bed, I lay down on the couch until Trinity decides to wake up from her nap. A few hours pass and it's time to at least start putting on our clothes. I make sure my house is clean and disinfect it down with Lysol because of how many people were here last night and I do have an infant I don't need getting sick. Six o' clock is here already. I stop cleaning, start pumping milk and making bottles for tonight. I think it's time to start making Trinity some bottles with baby food and cereal in it. Thirty minutes after pumping and making bottles, I make sure I look ready to go and double check Trinity's diaper bag again.

Evan has never been to my new house. I don't feel like driving today and I didn't get my full eight hours of sleep. I don't wanna risk driving today with my baby in the car. I look over at the clock when I hear a knock at the door at 6:45 p.m.

"Damn you're fifthteen minutes early. What, you came to tour my house before we go?"

"Aye aye aye, please don't start tonight okay."

"I'm just playing with you, relax Dr. King."

We head out exactly at seven and make our way to this restaurant I used to love going to when we were together. Once we are seated, I take off my jacket and make myself comfortable. He automatically spots the necklace on my neck. He didn't say anything about it, but I see him smiling from the corner of my eye. The waiter takes our order and it takes our food no longer than twenty minutes to come out. Evan starts a conversation about plans for the summer. I don't want to be negative or try to turn down all of his plans.

"Alex and I are a thing now and I really like him. I want you to be able to do things with Trinity this summer, but not always with me included."

"Okay no problem, that's fine. I'm just here to let you know some of the things I have planned for the summer, you can pick and choose what you want to be a part of and if he's going to be around my daughter, then I guess you can maybe include him in some activities too."

"Oh wow and I guess you can bring whoever you're seeing around too. We'll all have fun."

"Ever since you left, I haven't been with anyone. I haven't looked at anyone either because I always hoped you'd come back and give me a second chance. Pretty stupid of me to think that."

"It's not stupid, but I've never given anyone a second chance to disappoint me in my entire life."

"But you wouldn't know if I would have disappointed you twice because you didn't give me that chance to prove myself Aneese. I would've made things right for us."

I look down in my lap with my head down. I don't know if he wants me to feel bad or something, but I do. I pick my head up and start to look around. I see this lady looking at me rolling her eyes from three tables away. I start laughing so hard. Wow, these days I've been laughing out loud a lot but it's always for some negative shit. Evan looks at me and asks what's funny. I tell him to look three tables away. He turns around and looks, sis waves at him with her neck tilted to the side. She then walks over to the table. Here goes that face expression he likes to make. Damn, we just got here and are already running into some shit.

"Are you not going to acknowledge me and your son Evan?"

"Um that's not his baby, so move along before we all get kicked out of this restaurant because if he didn't already tell you I'm going to let you know right now I'm not the one to play games with."

"I wasn't talking to you, now was I?"

"I'm talking to you though and you're interrupting my family time."

I see Evan sitting there smiling as little Miss. Tiffany is getting upset about his silence. Little do she know he'll never come to her rescue even if that baby was his.

"Can you move away from this table, that's not my baby, I don't want you and never did. I would love to finish my night with my actual child and this beautiful lady right here, now bye."

She walks away with her baby in the stroller and all I can do is laugh. This is very funny to me. We're having a great dinner and this was the entertainment for the night. I needed that good old laugh. We get the check, Evan pays, and we leave. Evan turns on the GPS and puts in my address. I told him we'll sleep by him tonight if that's okay with him. Of course he would never say no. We get back to the apartment and put Trinity to bed. We cuddle up on the couch together. I began talking about her first birthday. This conversation is long overdue because I'm the extra parent and would like his input on ideas as well. He turns to me and says, "Tell me about this Alex dude. Is he better than me?"

I laugh and say, "He's not you and you're not him, we'll just leave it at that."

He smiles and wishes me luck in my relationship. Next thing I know we fall asleep and I wake up and it's morning already. Evan's walking around the house singing to Trinity and it is the cutest sight ever. I ask for a towel to wash my face before I head back home. It's Saturday, which is his time with Trinity. I can call Alex and have him pick me up instead of letting Evan drive me all the way back home with the baby. I text Alex asking if it was possible for him to pick me up. He asks for the address and tells me to give him about forty minutes.

Later that day

When Alex finally gets here to pick me up, he asks what I have planned for the day. I told him I didn't have anything planned besides going back home. He looks at me and says,

"How about we just drive somewhere, get a hotel and explore."

"What, I don't have any clothes or anything and it's early as hell."

"We can buy whatever we need along the way. Just say yes and we'll just keep driving."

I say yes and pull my seat all the way back and close my eyes. I wake up an hour later and press my head against the window. I see nothing but trees and roads. This should be very interesting. Knowing Alex, I'd say he planned this before today. He likes to explore and go on adventures. This would probably explain why he doesn't have any children momentarily, but I do have a child. She's not even a toddler yet and even though he seems very cool about me having an infant, I still feel like I'm holding him back in many ways. My child comes first and before anything. I don't want there to be a time when he secretly surprises me with a trip or date and I have to decline because my child is sick or something of that nature.

Okay enough of this, I don't need my mind doing this to me right now. I want to explore and enjoy whatever he has planned for us this weekend, that's it. Every time something is flowing perfectly, I start overthinking and thinking the absolute worst. I hate it and I'm sick of it. Why can't I just be happy for myself? I can't be normal for a whole day. Why can't I accept the fact that I deserve everything good that comes to me? Shit.

Alex pulls up to this shopping area and opens my door. I get out and look around trying to figure where the hell he took me. He grabs my hand and we walk into a clothing store. He kisses on my cheek and tells me to go shopping and not to worry about the price tags. Just because he told me not to worry about the price, I'm going to look at every tag in the store.

"Bae, I'm going to run in the shoe store next door, I'll be back."

I smile and keep looking through the clothing racks. This is cute and all, but I love to overpack when I know I'm not coming back home for a night. Imagine how I feel leaving for the weekend with nothing but my purse. Let me stop complaining for once and just pick out some clothes. I found four different outfits, two for outside activities and two for dinner. I don't know what Alex is up to yet, but I can guarantee he will come back to this store with some sort of shoes for me. I don't want to complain or seem ungrateful, but this is a bit too much. I think after this weekend, we need to take a little break on things. He walks back into the store and hands me a bag. Ughhh, I knew it. I take the bag and he takes the clothes out of my hand and heads over to the counter to pay for them. He then takes me to this little shop up the road to pick out new panties and bras. He stays in the car and hands me his card. This store is beautiful and I wont act shy to pick things up this time. On my way to the counter, I see this beautiful silk dress. It was perfect, not too long, not too short. I have to have it, Alex has to see me in it and I'm buying it along with all this other stuff. After leaving the store, he pulls up in front of a door. I know it's a hotel room, but he already had the room key. See, I knew he had this all planned out, I'm not going to say a word. He gets out and opens my door. He opens the door and allows men to walk in first. There were rose petals everywhere and to be honest, the way the outside looks, I would've never guessed the inside of this room looked this nice. Tears started to drop from my eyes as I turned around and hugged him.

"Aww, come here my big baby."

I'm speechless right now. If this man wanted to marry me this very second I probably would say yes in the heat of the moment. We settle in and freshen up. He then asks me if I ever went hiking. I look at him and say,

"No, do you not see these pretty feet, they have never walked up a dangerous mountain for hours."

"We today's you and your pretty feet's lucky day because that's first on the list."

"So, you think because you planned that for today I'm gonna go hiking."

Two hours later, I'm hiking up a mountain. I would've never agreed to go hiking if Evan ever brought it up. Another two hours passes us by and we're finally at the top of the mountain. It's so beautiful up here and very high up. I feel like we're a step away from the clouds. Like I can grab a piece of it and put it in my pocket. We take some pictures and make our way back down to the bottom. I nearly had a panic attack five times coming down. I thought I was going to die and never get to see my baby again.

We finally get back to the hotel and there's a table inside with covered dinner plates on it.

"Okay so now is the perfect time to ask what's the occasion? I didn't say anything about the drive, the shopping, you giving me your card and already booking a hotel room and acting like you woke up and wanted to just take a drive."

"I'm just trying to show you my appreciation, nothing more, nothing less."

"I don't believe you, you're up to something and I'll advise you to stop trying to fuck with me."

"Positive energy sweetheart. We're exploring together and having fun. I don't see anything wrong with that. It's better than staying in the house and not doing anything at all. Why sit home separately and text when we can be out having a good time together?"

"Umhmm, whatever you say."

We sit down and eat dinner and I'm beginning to feel like this is way too much. We're moving too fast and once again I'm going along with everything in front of me. I didn't like the outcome of me going along with things the first time with Evan and I sure as hell don't want to make the same mistake with someone else. Today's the last day of me going along with what someone else wants. Tomorrow I'm going to take charge of my life again and I want to go home. The rest of the night was awkward because I don't want to do anything else. I feel uncomfortable now. We watched TV in silence until Alex decided he wanted to start a conversation. We're talking and he takes my hand and reassures me I can talk to him about whatever's bothering me. I turn my head and stare into his eyes for five whole minutes in silence.

"I keep telling myself this is all too much, then I tried to convince myself this is what I finally deserved. I don't think I'm ready for all this. I feel like I'm just going along with everything because maybe I'm still kind of hurt by all the things I've been through in my life."

"I totally understand and I kind of figured maybe you still had a lot of hurt bottled up inside of you. That's why I go above and beyond for you. You've been through a lot in your life and never had someone to honestly depend on. I see a lot of sad things when I look into your eyes. Whatever we have going on here, it happened naturally. We're still friends before anything. I just want you to be happy."

"This is why I have so much love for you. You're perfect, too perfect and I'm very broken. I see that now."

"It's okay, I see a fighter when I look into your eyes. You'll blossom into a whole new person soon. Believe me when I tell you. I apologize if I pushed myself on you too hard, I was only trying to make you feel good in every way possible. I can take you home tonight if that's what you want."

"You've made me feel good in every way possible. That shit scares me and makes me overthink all day long. That's how I knew I wasn't ready to jump into another relationship right now. And it's already late, I can go home tomorrow."

"No problem hun. I'll always be here if you ever need me. I'll never walk away from you or ignore you in your time of need, remember that."

I smile at him and kiss him on the cheek. He stares at me, takes both of my hands and kisses them. He walked over to the couch with a pillow and a blanket.

"You don't have to lay on the couch, I actually would love to be held tonight."

He walks back over to the bed and puts his pillow back on his side of the bed. I go put on the night dress I bought earlier today and slip into the bed. Alex cuddles up behind me and whispers I'm beautiful in my ear and not long after he was snoring. I don't know what planet this man was created on, but I would love to thank God for taking his time creating this wonderful person. Tomorrow's the day I'll point out all of my bad habits and work on them one by one. I'm going to plan out more activities with the girls and try my very best to live a positive life. That means co-parenting with Evan without all the arguing and negativity I bring to the table. I'm going to be greater from here on out.

My name is Aneese Myers and I am a victim of sexual abuse. I would like to call myself a living survivor. Not everyone gets to keep their life after being raped. Not only was I raped one time, but I was raped twice in my life. No, I am not ashamed of my story. No, it's not my fault. No, I did not allow my childhood and adult trauma to control my future. Yes, I've been depressed, felt alone, and even, at times, thought it was all my fault. Guess what, it wasn't my fault and I am still standing strong today. I am beautiful and I'm alive! I came out of the storm dancing and I'm here to try and help everyone else dance out of their storm too.

Epilogue

Months after I found great happiness in my life doing everything I was meant to do, I learned how to forgive for real this time. I went many years thinking I forgave people because I said those words out my mouth plenty of times and I thought those thoughts all day long. I tried to train my mind to believe that lie, but I was still very angry and couldn't figure out why. Learning true forgiveness has molded me into being one of the greatest women in the world to everyone I know. I graduated college with my masters and kept my promise to all the girls I've helped in my #Metoo group. We created a family together, I bonded with them, made myself available at all times for them and gave them things they felt they never had in life. All it took was a listening ear, understanding and a little love that eventually turned into unconditional love. I would also love to give them credit for helping make me a better person today. One day I woke and wrote an amazing book about my life that included all the challenges I've faced, how to stay strong through trauma, and how to truly forgive the people that hurt you. You will never be truly happy if you don't learn how to forgive your abuser because walking around angry and acting out is kind of telling your attacker they still have power over your every move.

The book blew up bigger than I expected, but I was truly grateful and had everyone I loved by my side. I traveled the world while making a difference and continued to be the best mom I could be to Trinity. I was finally the person she's going to grow up and be very proud of. My second biggest accomplishment after having my child was me pointing out all the negativity in my life, facing it and tackling it. Therapy was helpful only on those days I went, but true healing is beyond sitting down talking about your feelings or drawing out feelings with a color pencil. You have to really ask yourself what are you going to do about these feelings and the way you behave? I wanted true happiness and now I have it.

You may wonder if Alex and I still keep in contact, yes we do. Even though we dated for a few months, I enjoyed every moment we had together. He always came over to help me study, he even started cooking for me. We went on weekly dates and he still paid for everything. On graduation day he sent so many dozens of roses to my house because he knew that was my favorite flower and wanted me to know how proud of me he was. I never asked this man for anything, but he always sent me things and made me smile. Who wouldn't love a guy like that? He was the perfect guy, but just not for me. He understood and meant it when he said he wanted to be friends in the beginning. He definitely brought positivity and love into my life at a sad time. Because of our short history, I promised to always love Alex and would never trade our friendship for nothing or no one. Maybe in another life we'll find each other sooner than we did in this one. If he's the same man, I wouldn't mind it.

I've made all the right decisions for my life in such a short amount of time and now I'm a very well known author, successful, and living my best life. Lets not skip over the part where I'm a wonderful mother of not just one but two beautiful girls. Who's the father? Evan's the father once again. While growing as a person and always bumping heads, somewhere along the way I decided to give Evan a second chance for Trinity's sake and because we still loved each other. It just took me a little while to see that I did still love him and all that anger made me think otherwise. After being back together for maybe a week, Evan proposed to me again. This time I didn't even bother to hesitate. I said yes because why not? We've already been through so much and I think he learned his lesson for taking me for granted once. Shit, that man is lost without me, but I was never lost without him, so who really has the power? Me, I have the power. I had to learn that when shit hits the fan, I can't just walk away from everything and give up on it. What kind of person would I be today if I continued that behavior. Everything in your life happens for a reason whether it's good or bad, so I wouldn't want to change nothing that happened in my life. I've accepted all the bad that happened to me, but if I had the chance to know why I would love to know. But right now I'm just grateful for all the closure I was able to get and I know my mom is smiling down at me letting me know she's proud of who I am today. Maybe my dad is furious down there because he couldn't break me with his sickness, but I forgive him too. Therefore, this was my happy ending I always hoped for and it was granted to me with time, growth and patience.

About The Author

My name is Kiltalya Washington and I see myself as one of the definitions of a Strong Black young woman. I grew up in Brooklyn, New York where I faced many traumas in my life. I spent more than my entire life feeling alone, depressed, and angry. Writing was always my happy place and the pieces of paper was the only thing I could honestly talk to. I've been writing stories since the third grade. November 2016, The current story (The Life I've Lived) was started, but was put on pause for many years because I tried to forget the hurt I've been through. I was put in a situation that led me into a deeper depression than I was already in. I felt traumatized all over again. I went to sleep that night and had a dream similar to the situation that occurred that day, but just saw it happen differently. I woke up and started to feel tired of feeling tired and unhappy. Opened a notebook and wrote one paragraph of "dialogue" between a husband and wife who started to hate each other. That part represented what was going on with a current boyfriend. I started to think about all the bad things I'd been through as a child and knew I had a story to tell without having to write over 200 pages of words with no meaning. People were always quick to judge me and talk about the bad attitude I had, but no one took the time to ask why I was so angry. But eventually good things began to happen for me, my mental health, and my life overall. With time I worked on me all by myself. My next steps were to finish writing this story and to be an emotional supporter to anyone who's in need of it. I want everyone who feels alone to know they're not alone, there's always someone with a listening ear and an understanding heart and "YOUR LIFE IS NOT OVER".

Acknowledgements

I would love to give a special thanks to "13 & Joan" for helping me on my first great achievement. Thank you for helping make a dream come true.

I would also like to give thanks to a former academic coach by the name of "Constance Del Valle". From a small dialogue to an entire page, she would always allow me to come meet with her to go through whatever I wrote to make corrections and any sort of changes. She'd give me suggestions whether I liked them or not. When I felt like giving up, she never allowed me to give up myself or anything else. She always supported me and for that I thank her.

Lastly, I would like to give thanks to myself thanks for completing my book with good intentions and to any and everyone that ever sent me messages and trusted me enough to confide in me . I don't want no young girl, boy, man, or woman to allow their past trauma or current trauma to take over their life, mind, and mental state that can lead into darkness. And a special thanks to anyone who felt safe to share their stories with me.

CONNECT WITH AUTHOR ON SOCIAL MEDIA

Instagram (@Kiltalya_Washington)
Twitter (@KiltalyaW)
Facebook (@KiltalyaWashington)
Linkedin (@KiltalyaWashington)
Tumblr (@dontcryvol1)

www.ingramcontent.com/pod-product-compliance
Lightning Source LLC
Chambersburg PA
CBHW071509070526
44578CB00001B/483